THE THRILL OF JETS

So what is it that makes jets so fascinating? Why do we always wish we were up there when we see those white **vapour trails** in the clear blue sky? Why do we get such a thrill simply from hearing a jet roar overhead? It is simply because they are fast. Brain-thumpingly, mind-numbingly fast!

All these thrills and sheer excitement come at a price. Jet engines are expensive pieces of equipment. They can cost millions to design, produce and develop. They cost a fortune to buy, too. **Private jets** are only for the super-rich!

Which jet broke the sound barrier?

How do jump-jets take off?

Which jets are invisible?

vapour trail   white trail left in the sky by a jet

5

WHAT IS A JET?

People can fly in balloons, gliders and aeroplanes. The most common way to fly is by jet aircraft.

Jets have been around for about 50 years, but the first experiments started long ago. Jets have changed the world because we can now get around so quickly.

HOW JETS WORK

Jet engines suck in air at the front and force it out of the back. They force it out much faster than they suck it in. That is what makes the plane move forward.

THE FIRST EXPERIMENT

Experiments done in 1791 helped to make jets like the one below possible. John Barberin used spinning fans to produce a jet of gas. This was the first jet engine experiment, but no engine was built. The metals available at this time were not suitable.

compressor   part of a jet engine that squeezes the air going through the engine

Powerful fans, called **compressors**, squeeze the air as it goes through the engine. The air is then mixed with fuel and exploded by a spark.

The heat from this explosion makes the air **expand** quickly. To escape, it shoots out from the back of the engine very quickly. On its way, it passes through the **turbine**. This is what we call a 'jet' engine.

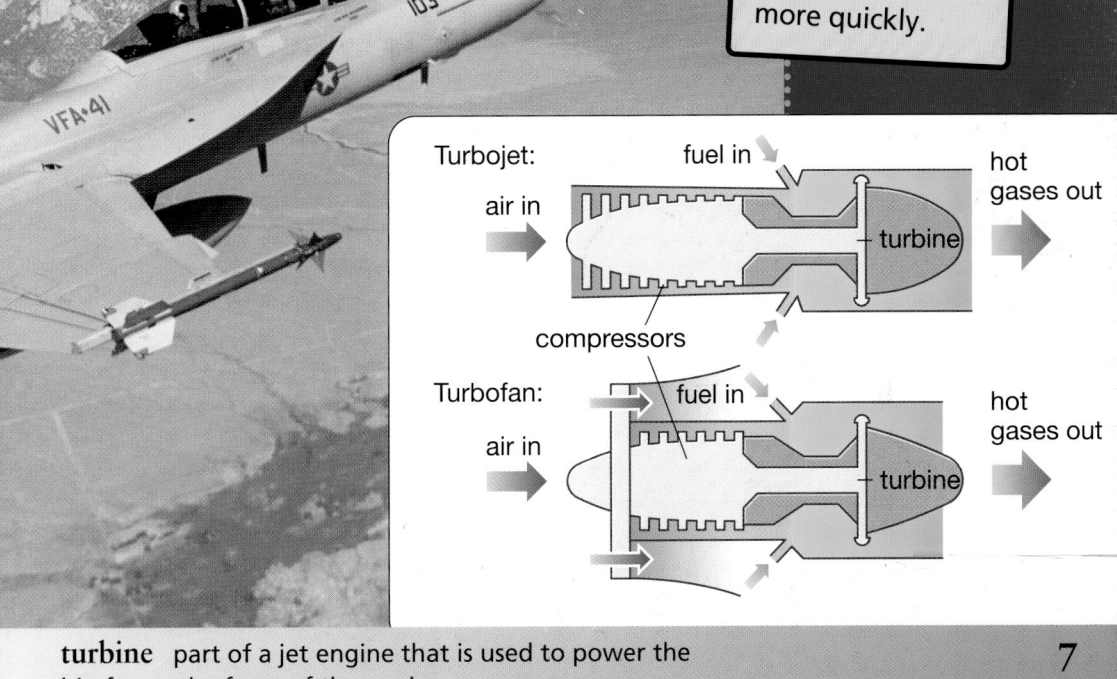

turbine   part of a jet engine that is used to power the big fan at the front of the engine

7

THE FIRST JETS

In 1937, a young Englishman called Frank Whittle built the first jet engine. It was an experiment, but the start of World War 2 in 1939 made people take jet engines far more seriously. Scientists realised that if jet engines could be made to work, their side would have an advantage in the war.

Although Whittle built the first engine, German scientists soon caught up with him. By 1945, the Germans had built a number of jet aircraft, including the Arado Ar 234, the Heinkel He 162, the Me 262 and the Me 163. The British only had one jet aircraft, the Gloster Meteor, and the Americans had none at all.

ME 163 KOMET

Some early jet planes looked odd. The Me 163 Komet was the first ever jet fighter. It broke the world air speed record. Unfortunately, it had a nasty habit of blowing up when it was landing because the engine was **unstable**.

Frank Whittle (right) is the father of all jet aircraft.

THE JET RACE

After World War 2 ended in 1945 a great race started between the Soviet Union (now Russia), Britain and the USA to increase the power and speed of their fighter jets. The German scientists who built jets during the war were now helping everyone else.

The first results of this race were the USA's F-86 Sabre, the Soviet MiG-15 and Britain's Hawker Hunter. Sweden also developed the Saab J29. By the early 1950s, bombers were being built that were just as fast, such as the American B-45 Tornado and the British Canberra.

Jets were developed too late to have a big effect on World War 2. They had a big effect in later years, though.

ME 262

The best of the early jets was the German Me 262, which was years ahead of its time. It was developed too late to help Germany win World War 2.

MAKING JETS

A jet engine takes about two years to build. That is longer than it takes to build the aircraft the engines will power! The parts are made to the highest standards from the best materials. Companies that build jets can employ as many as 40,000 people. That is because the engines are very complicated. The engine of a Boeing 747 has 25,000 parts. Making a jet is not an easy task. It takes a great deal of planning.

TECH TALK

Jet engine building records
- Most powerful: General Electric GE90-115B
- Biggest: General Electric GE90-115B
- Smallest: Williams International FJ22
- World's only **vertical** take-off and landing jet: Rolls-Royce Pegasus
- Most common: Pratt and Whitney JT8D

These Rolls Royce mechanics are highly skilled.

TECH TALK

The world's biggest makers of jet engines are:
- General Electric (USA)
- Pratt and Whitney (USA)
- Rolls-Royce (UK)

vertical   straight up (and down)

TESTING, TESTING

Once the engine is built, it must be tested. Every part of the engine must pass many different tests before it can be used. The engine is run for many hours non-stop, in all sorts of weather conditions. It is examined in a **wind tunnel** and inspected by experts. Dead birds are even fired at the fan blades, because birds are sometimes sucked into the engine when planes take off. Small explosions are set off inside the engine as part of the testing. This checks that the case will not crack if parts shatter inside.

The parts that make up a jet engine are built all over the world.

wind tunnel   place where testing can be done on speed and conditions

11

The Pegasus X-47A is currently at prototype stage.

TESTING NEW JETS

Even with computer **simulations**, there is still a need for test pilots. These are brave, daring men and women who fly new aircraft with untested technology. No one knows if the jets will actually work in the air. Test pilots go up and find out.

BRAVE OR BARMY?

Some people think test pilots have to be a bit crazy. They push their experimental planes harder, higher and faster than they are supposed to go. Without these pilots, ordinary people would not enjoy the safety in the air that we have today.

Being a test pilot is very risky. Many have died making aircraft safer for us.

PROTOTYPES

Before any aircraft can go into service, it must be tested. The planes that are tested are called **prototypes**. These prototypes help to show up any problems before the aircraft is flown in **combat** or used to carry passengers.

TECH TALK

Many famous test pilots flew from Edwards Air Force Base in California. The base is named after Glen Edwards, who was killed during a test in 1948. All the roads around the base are named after pilots who died in test flights.

drag   when air pushes back against an aircraft and slows it down

An aeroplane's nose is shaped to cut through air smoothly.

HEROES

The **golden age** for test pilots was after World War 2 and into the 1950s. Testing the new jet engines was exciting but dangerous work.

Hannah Reitsch was the main German test pilot during the war. She flew the first manned rocket and tested early helicopter designs. After the war, American test pilots such as Chuck Yeager and Scott Crossfield flew planes that went faster and faster. At this time, **sonic booms** were often heard in the sky. The pilots were pushing harder and harder. They are pushing just as hard today.

TOP SPEED

The highest speeds can only be achieved with **streamlining**. Modern aircraft are designed so they move through the air quickly, with very little **drag**.

sonic boom noise heard when an aircraft passes by at a speed faster than Mach 1

BREAKING THE BARRIER

The early jets broke speed records regularly. Then came a big problem. Jets started having trouble. Aircraft would shake mysteriously and many crashed, killing their pilots. In 1952, 62 test pilots died in 36 weeks. Scientists knew the problem was to do with the speed of sound, but they could not work out what to do.

BELL X-1

The first **supersonic** plane was the Bell X-1. It broke the sound barrier in 1947. The plane was dropped from the bomb doors of a larger plane, because the X-1 could not take off on its own. The pilot fired up the rocket engine and off he sped.

This DH-108 experimental plane crashed in 1950, killing the pilot.

Mach 1   the speed of sound
supersonic   faster than the speed of sound

SONIC BOOM

When a plane flies faster than sound travels, air in front of it cannot move out of the way quickly enough. It builds up into a shock wave, like the wave of water in front of a ship. The shock wave spreads out, just like ripples on water. When the wave rushes past someone on the ground, they hear a large booming noise – the **sonic boom**. This was the only barrier stopping jets going faster.

Once Chuck Yeager broke the **sound barrier**, planes kept getting faster and faster.

TECH TALK

The pilot who first broke the sound barrier was Chuck Yeager. The night before the flight, Yeager fell off a horse and broke two ribs. He kept quiet about his accident because he did not want to miss making the flight.

sound barrier   drag and other problems that make a plane hard to control when it gets close to the speed of sound

X-PLANES

X-Planes are experimental aircraft. These experiments try to create improvements in performance and design.

Many of today's famous planes started life as an X-Plane experiment. Without the X-Planes there would be no **stealth planes** and Concorde would never have flown.

INTO THE UNKNOWN

X-Plane pilots were very brave. They were the ones who tried out new things, never knowing what might go wrong. Many of these test pilots lost their lives making things safer for today's jet passengers.

X-Planes were designed to do many different things. Some were built for speed, others for very high **altitudes**. Some X-Planes were even built just to try out new engines.

THE GOBLIN

The Goblin was a plane carried inside a bomber. If the bomber was attacked, the Goblin was lowered through the bomb doors and launched. Once it had driven away the enemy, the Goblin would hook back on to the bomber, fold up its wings and be pulled back inside.

The Goblin was first dropped from a US bomber in 1948.

altitude   height above sea level

STRANGE MACHINES

One thing is certain – many X-Planes looked really odd! But their purpose was to experiment, not to look pretty.

X-Planes were flown from Edwards Air Force base in California, one of the most famous airfields in the world. It was chosen because it is so far away from towns and cities. The experiments could remain a secret.

The X-Planes are not very well known. Without them there would be no **supersonic** flight or even space travel.

U.S. AIR FORCE

They look odd, but modern planes depend on these experiments.

SWING-WING

Swing-wing aircraft have the best of both worlds. With their wings swept back they are able to fly super-fast. Bringing the wings into the straight position means the plane can turn more sharply and take off more easily.

TECH TALK

The first man to walk on the Moon was Neil Armstrong. He was also an X-Plane test pilot.

stealth plane   aircraft that is difficult to detect with radar

PUSHING THE LIMITS

X-Planes explore what it is possible for an aircraft to do. Quite often these aircraft look unusual. The Grumman X-29A is one of these. It looks like it is flying backwards.

The X-29A was the first serious attempt at a **supersonic** aircraft with wings swept forwards. Forward wings had been tried in the 1940s. It was hoped these wings would be stronger than traditional wings. The problem was that the wings had to be thin, or else the aircraft was difficult to control.

X-31

The X-31 is a **test-bed** jet. It can fly at **angles of attack** that would make other jets **stall** and go out of control. Technology tested on the X-31 will be a part of future fighter aircraft.

angle of attack   how high the nose of the aircraft points upwards /downwards during flight

MODERN MATERIALS

The best materials only became available in the 1970s and 1980s. The metals must be extremely strong but very light. The X-29A tried out many different sorts of materials.

X-Planes have tried and tested many different ideas. They have tested new engines, even solar-powered ones. They have tried out new designs and new weapons. They have experimented with high **altitudes** and super-low flying. If something is part of a real jet plane, it is a good bet that it was once tried out on an X-Plane.

X-35

The X-35 tests short take-offs and landings. It also tries out new **vertical** take off technology. The lessons learned testing the X-35 will be used to make the new JSF – Joint Strike Fighter. The aim is to build the best **combat** aircraft in the world.

TECH TALK

Grumman X-29A:
technical data
- First flight: 1984
- Length: 48.1 m
- Wingspan: 27.2 m
- Top speed: **Mach** 1.6
- Maximum altitude: 50,000 feet

IN THE COCKPIT

If you want to fly an aircraft there are a number of ways to do it. Many young people join the **Air Cadets**. Teenagers learn all about flying aircraft and even get the chance to learn to fly themselves.

FLYING FOR A LIVING

You could also join the Air Force. This does not always mean you will actually get to fly yourself, because there are thousands of different jobs to do. Only the very best get chosen to train as pilots in the Air Force. You would have to pass many tests and examinations.

GOING SOLO

When a pilot learns to fly, the instructor is right behind the learner in the plane. Unlike a driving test, pilots only pass when they fly 'solo', with no one else on board.

Air Cadets   youth organization whose members learn about aircraft

AIRLINE PILOTS

Some airlines choose to train their own pilots. You could learn to fly by getting a place on an airline training scheme. Once again, only the very best are chosen and there are only a small number of places. Competition is very tough.

BACK TO SCHOOL

You could pay for flying lessons yourself at a private flying school. Many adults do this and learn to fly for fun. If you want to learn to fly jets, you will need lots of money. Jet aircraft are expensive to own and run, which means that lessons are expensive too.

UNDER PRESSURE

When a fighter plane turns sharply, blood flows from the pilot's brain. Pilots can even **black out**. To prevent this, pilots wear special pressure suits. These suits squeeze the pilot's legs, which stops blood draining down.

black out lose consciousness for a few seconds

LEARNING TO FLY

Training a jet pilot is a long and expensive job. Only people with excellent health are chosen for training.

PRACTICE MAKES PERFECT

Pilot training is very realistic. Pilots spend many hours in flight **simulators**. This is so they can learn to fly without any of the dangers. Crashing a plane in a simulator means you still walk away alive! The simulators can be programmed to copy many different problems and situations.

Using flight simulators can also save money. They do not need a team of mechanics and engineers to look after them, either.

LINK TRAINER

Because flying lessons were expensive, in the 1930s Edward Link invented the first training machine for use on the ground. His machine copied the movement of an aircraft. The trainee pilot never had to leave the ground. The idea soon caught on.

The Hawk can fly faster than Mach 1 in a dive.

flight deck   in a passenger aircraft, the place where the pilot sits

THE HAWK TRAINER

Eventually jet pilots have to get into the air. The plane is most likely to be a Hawk trainer jet. This is the main training jet used by air forces around the world.

The Hawk is reliable and cheap to fly. It can also be refuelled very quickly. It has two seats – one for the pilot and one for the instructor.

The Hawk is also good for training pilots to use weapons. It can carry training cannons, practice bombs, missiles and rocket launchers. The Hawk is even used by experienced pilots who are training to land on aircraft carrier ships.

FLIGHT SIMULATORS

Modern flight simulators are run by computers. They can be made to look just like the **flight deck** of any real aircraft. They are able to copy many different weather conditions, dangerous situations and emergencies. Pilots spend many hours in these training simulators.

simulator   a training machine that imitates flight

FLIGHT DECK

The **flight deck** is where the captain and co-pilot of a **jetliner** sit. The controls and instruments that they need during the flight are here. These tell the captain about speed, height, direction and so on. The knobs, dials, levers and display panels are complex, but the basic controls have not changed much since the early days of flying.

COMPUTER DISPLAYS

The latest jets show information on computer screens. The pilot is told everything from airspeed and **altitude** to whether the windscreen wipers are working properly. These are clearer to look at and more reliable than old-fashioned dials and pointers.

OPEN COCKPIT

The first aircraft usually had an open control area with a windshield to keep off the rush of air during flight. Controls were very simple.

TECH TALK

Flight deck or cockpit? These are both terms for the control area of an aircraft. In small planes it is a **cockpit**. In large planes it is a flight deck.

cockpit   in a combat aircraft, the place where the pilot sits
stick   control lever that changes the direction of a plane

FLIGHT CONTROLS

Moving a central **stick** left or right rolls the plane from side to side. Moving it back or forwards pitches the plane up or down. Many jetliners and **combat** jets have a side-stick instead of one in the middle, but it works in a similar way.

Foot pedals work the rudder, which is used for making adjustments in the turns. The engine power is controlled by a **throttle** that increases or reduces **thrust**.

Training pilots spend as much time in the classroom as in the air.

The flight deck of a passenger jet.

CHECKLIST

One thing that has not changed in a century of flight is the pre-flight checklist. Before take-off, a pilot goes through a list to make sure all the systems are working. Every pilot has to spend a long time learning all this information.

thrust force produced by a jet engine to push a plane forward

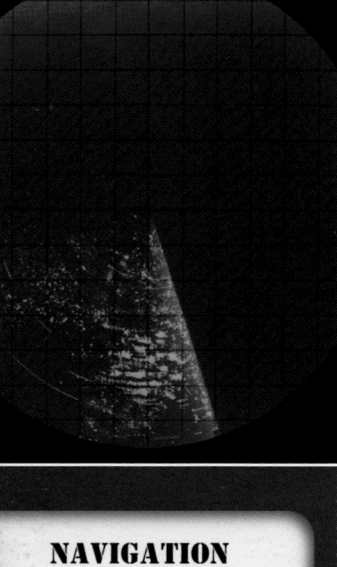

COMMUNICATIONS

The **cockpits** of modern jet aircraft are full of controls, dials and flashing lights. It seems almost impossible that anyone could know what they all mean. But the pilots do!

IN CONTROL

There are many controls and dials that are to do with basic flight control. There also many more that deal with **navigation**, **hydraulics**, engine condition, weather, **radar** and radio communications. As the skies are full of aircraft today, pilots must make sure their communication is good. Ignoring the radio or the radar could mean disaster.

NAVIGATION

Modern jets carry an incredible range of technology. Navigation is done electronically with help from radar and satellites. The equipment is accurate to a few metres and can also see any dangers, including bad weather.

Air traffic controllers are in constant communication with pilots.

hydraulics strong equipment that uses liquid under pressure to move heavy parts of the airplane smoothly

MODERN COCKPITS

Computers now control many of an aircraft's systems. This means that screens called CRTs (Cathode Ray Tubes) are replacing the dials and lights. The pilot can change the information on the screen at the press of a button.

KEEPING IN TOUCH

An aircraft must have good communication with staff on the ground. Being in touch with them means the pilot can be warned about problems. Information about weather conditions is especially important. Radar also helps to spot dangers or hazards. It can tell the pilot if other aircraft are too close, or even if there is a storm ahead.

RADAR

Radar works by sending out radio waves and picking up any that are reflected back. A radar operator can tell where something is by the time it takes for the waves to bounce back.

Radar operators can warn of the first signs of danger.

radar (Radio Detection and Ranging) way of seeing other planes when they are several miles away

EMERGENCY

Fighter jets cost many millions of pounds to build. You cannot put a cost on the people who fly them, though. Fighter crews are very important, as they take years to train. They must be protected.

WHEN THINGS GO WRONG

If the crew have to get out of a fighter jet, they use the ejector seat. They pull a handle and the hatch of the aircraft automatically blows away. Then a rocket fires under the seat and the pilot is shot out into the air, clear of the danger. All this happens in under half a second. The pilot never even leaves the seat! The pilot and seat float down to the ground under a parachute.

In crashes like this, an ejector seat gives the pilot a good chance of survival.

signal beacon   device that sends out an emergency radio signal

EQUIPMENT EVERYWHERE

All pilots wear life preservers. These automatically inflate if the pilot parachutes into water. Flight crew also wear survival jackets that contain an amazing amount of equipment.

No pilot wants to eject from an aircraft, but sometimes they have no choice. The emergency systems built into their plane, their seat and their clothes will all help to keep them safe.

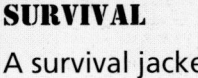

In some planes, pilots can eject safely at ground level.

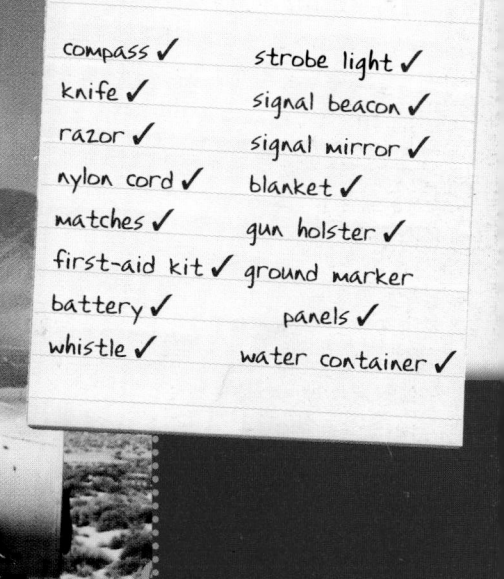

SURVIVAL

A survival jacket contains:

compass ✓	strobe light ✓
knife ✓	signal beacon ✓
razor ✓	signal mirror ✓
nylon cord ✓	blanket ✓
matches ✓	gun holster ✓
first-aid kit ✓	ground marker
battery ✓	panels ✓
whistle ✓	water container ✓

strobe light powerful flashing light used to signal for help

ACCIDENTS HAPPEN

Accidents are rare on **jetliners** but emergencies can sometimes happen. Modern jetliners have many built-in safety features. Smoke and flame detectors protect engines and mechanical parts. These instantly set off **extinguishers** if fire breaks out. All systems have back-ups and the computer will stop the pilot flying dangerously.

PRACTICE MAKES PERFECT

Cabin crew normally pour drinks or help passengers. They are still prepared for emergencies and know exactly what to do. They go through many training **simulations** during their training and have to know how to deal with dangerous situations.

SAFETY MYTH

When an aircraft crashes it is a big story. It can give people the idea that jets are unsafe. This is not true. On average, a pilot can expect to be in an accident every 400 years!

Despite occasional crashes like this one at Milan Airport in 2001, air travel remains safer than travelling by road.

extinguisher   fire-fighting cylinder kept on aircraft for emergencies

JUST IN CASE

A jetliner is also packed with personal safety equipment, including:

- oxygen masks that drop down from above the passengers in an emergency
- life rafts that inflate themselves quickly in case of an emergency sea landing
- blow-up escape slides to allow passengers to exit quickly and safely during an emergency
- medical equipment, life jackets, smaller extinguishers, survival rations and emergency navigation kits are all stored on board.

Every passenger's life jacket contains more safety equipment. They all have a **signal beacon** and a whistle to alert search parties. Thankfully emergencies are rare, but every jetliner is prepared for them.

This black box was recovered from a Swissair crash in 1998.

Cabin crew demonstrate safety equipment on every passenger jet flight.

BLACK BOX

Modern jetliners carry a 'black box' or Flight Data Recorder. The box records everything that happens during a flight. Black boxes are difficult to destroy, and are used to investigate accidents.

jetliner   jet plane built to carry passengers in comfort

COMMERCIAL JETS

Ever since the 1950s, the **jetliner** has transformed air travel. **Propeller planes** were fast for their time, but the powerful jets flew much faster. Great speeds could now be achieved and great distances could be flown. The jetliner also made air travel possible for everyone. Before the 1950s, only the very rich could afford to fly. Now millions of people fly all over the world every day.

BOEING 777

The Boeing 777 first flew in 1994. It is the largest twin-engined airliner in the world. It is so big that its engines are wider than a bus!

TECH TALK

The De Havilland Comet was the world's first jetliner. The Comet changed the face of air travel. The first Comets were involved in some tragic accidents, however, and companies like Boeing began to take over.

propeller plane   plane that is moved by a set of blades that spin round very quickly

HIGHER AND SMOOTHER

Flying is much more comfortable in a jetliner. Jets can fly high above any bad weather. Most propeller planes cannot do this. Their passengers have to put up with a much bumpier ride.

Flying high above bad weather means that the air pressure drops and the air becomes very thin. Jetliner passengers fly inside special pressurized cabins to protect them from the low air pressure.

Although today's jetliners look like 1950s machines, beneath the surface there have been many changes. Today's planes are much stronger, and are built with lighter materials. Computers **navigate** the plane and electronic systems control many other functions.

AIRBUS

This Airbus, an A320, can carry about 150 passengers. It cannot fly long distances, so is mainly used for short flights. It is wider and more comfortable than other, similar-sized jets.

◄ ◄ ◄ ◄ ◄ ◄ ◄ ◄ ◄ ◄ ◄ ◄
To find out more about the controls of jets, turn to pages 24–25.

Boeing 747: technical data
- First flight: 1969
- Length: 70.7 m
- Wingspan: 59.6 m
- Height: 19.3 m
- Passengers:
  452–568 people
- Range: 14,630 km
  (9144 miles)
- Cargo: 102,058 kg

MEGALINER

The Boeing 747 is the original 'Jumbo Jet'. It was given this nickname because it was massive compared to other planes. It was called a 'wide-body jet' because the main cabin is wide enough for ten seats and two aisles. There are also two passenger **decks,** as the plane is so tall.

Since 1970, Boeing 747s have carried 1.8 **billion** people more than 39.8 billion kilometres (24.7 billion miles).

billion   one thousand million

JUMBO BARGAINS

When the first Jumbo Jet went into service, many people wondered if it was just too big. Could enough passengers be found to fill it?

They certainly could! In fact, the Jumbo helped to make air travel affordable for millions of ordinary people. More passengers meant lower prices. The Jumbo is so popular that over 1100 have been built since 1970.

Some people call any big plane a 'Jumbo Jet'. But those who know anything about aircraft know that there is only one Jumbo: the Boeing 747.

A-380

The Airbus A-380 is even bigger than a Jumbo. The cabin has two passenger decks with two aisles down each one. Very few jets have flights of stairs inside.

TECH TALK

Airbus A380: technical data
- Length: 73 m
- Wingspan: 79.8 m
- Height: 24.1 m
- Passengers: 555–840 people
- Range: 14,800 km (9250 miles)
- A cargo version of the A380 has three decks!

decks floors

BUSINESS JETS

Private jets are most often used by people who are rich or in positions of power. Having your own jet means that you can go wherever you like with great speed. It also means you can travel when it suits you, not just when a flight is available from an airport. Private jets are very luxurious. They are almost like small hotels in the air.

ECLIPSE 500

The Eclipse 500 is a tiny jet that carries only six passengers. It is like a jet-taxi. It is cheap to own and run compared with many other private jets.

LUXURY LEARJETS

The most famous private jets are Learjets. They were first built by William Lear in the 1960s.

Learjets are designed to be able to fly in and out of small airfields. This gives passengers a greater choice of places to fly to. The big **jetliners** can only land at airports with massive runways.

TECH TALK

Learjet 45: technical data
- Length: 17.6 m
- Wingspan: 14.5 m
- Height: 4.3 m
- Passengers: 10
- Range: 3813 km (2383 miles)
- Top cruising speed: 859 km/h (534 mph)

LEARJET 45

Since the first Learjet, many different versions have been designed. The Learjet 45 is one of the most successful.

FIRST AND BEST

Many other companies build private jets, but Learjets are the most famous. A Learjet was the first private jet to fly around the world, travelling 36,996 km (22,993 miles) in just 50 hours and 20 minutes. It has broken many other records since. Its long range and high cruising **altitude** also made it popular and successful. Thousands of Learjets have been built since the 1960s.

GULFSTREAM

All private jets are expensive. But the Gulfstream is one of the most expensive of them all. The Gulfstream G500 has set world records for distance and speed. Each plane costs over US $40 million and can carry just nineteen passengers!

WEIGHTLIFTERS

When most people think of jet aircraft they think of warplanes or the planes that take them on holiday. But what about cargo planes?

These are planes that carry cargo all over the world. Without them there would be many changes to our lives. There would be no fresh strawberries or kiwi fruit in our supermarkets in the winter. If they had to travel by road or sea they would all be rotten by the time they reached us.

Cargo jets are huge and come in many strange shapes. The Airbus A300-600ST Beluga can carry very tall loads because it is so high and wide.

GLOBEMASTER

The Boeing C-17 Globemaster is a favourite military transport plane. It can carry hundreds of soldiers, or even three Apache helicopters. It is also the only aircraft that can parachute vehicles such as army jeeps.

The Airbus Beluga is named after the whale it looks like.

fuselage   main body of an aircraft

LOAD UP

We may not see cargo planes as often as the jets we use to go on holiday. No matter how big your holiday plane looks, remember that the cargo jets are the monsters of the air. The largest aircraft in the world are cargo planes.

Big cargo planes have to be carefully designed to carry huge weights. Crew must be careful when they load them. Cargo must be evenly spread through the aircraft or take-off could be dangerous. If too much weight is at one end of the plane, it could crash. Most of these planes have computer-loading systems to make sure everything is loaded correctly.

ANTONOV-225

This monster, the Antonov-225, is the biggest aircraft in the world. It can even carry a space shuttle on top of its **fuselage**. Only one has ever been built.

MILITARY JETS

Fighters are small, fast jets that are well-armed. Their main purpose is to attack and destroy other aircraft.

QUICK AND DEADLY

Modern fighters fly with the help of computers, but the pilot still uses a **stick**. When the stick moves, computers sense the movement and make the jet change direction. This is called fly-by-wire. Fighters like this can respond to the pilot with amazing speed. This way they are more likely to survive an air battle.

EUROFIGHTER

This Eurofighter Typhoon was designed and built by a partnership of countries: Germany, Spain, Italy and the UK. It looks set to become Europe's main fighter for decades to come.

The F-22, or Raptor, is the most advanced jet fighter in the US Air Force.

G-force   force of gravity that presses on pilots when they do sharp turns, steep climbs and dives

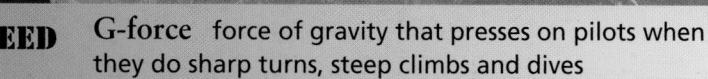

The F-16 Fighting Falcon was one of the first fly-by-wire fighters. The Fighting Falcon can perform amazingly tight turns, steep climbs and sharp dives. This means that pilots are forced back into their seats by the **G-force**. They feel ten times heavier than normal.

Fighters carry a range of weapons. They use guns to attack other aircraft as well as air-to-air missiles. They also carry heat-seeking missiles that can find a target and chase it.

Fighters often do other work too, such as attacking targets on the ground. Their main job is clearing the skies of enemy aircraft.

TECH TALK

Lockheed F-16 Fighting Falcon: technical data
- Length 15 m
- Wingspan: 9.4 m
- Height: 5.1 m
- Weapons: 20 mm cannon, AIM-7 Sparrow, AIM-9 Sidewinder, AMRAAM, Python 3, AGM shrike, AGM-65 Maverick
- Max speed: 1460 km/h (915 mph)
- Cost: US $20 million

JUMP JETS

Fighter jets need to speed along the ground quickly to take off. This is so that their wings can lift them up into the air. Jump jets are different.

STRAIGHT UP!

Jump jets do not need a runway. They can take off like a helicopter. This is called a **vertical** take-off. Jump jets are useful because they can take off from anywhere and be used for many different things. Because they do not need a runway they can land almost anywhere. Harriers can take off like a normal jet as well. In fact they often do, because a vertical take-off uses a lot of fuel.

JOINT STRIKE FIGHTER

The F-35 JSF (Joint Strike Fighter) is being designed at the moment. It should be in service by 2008. This jump jet will have stealth features and will become the main fighter of the US Air Force.

➤ ➤ ➤ ➤ ➤ ➤

Find out more about stealth features on pages 44–45.

THE ORIGINAL AND BEST

Even though there are other jump jets, the Harrier was the first to fly. It is still the most commonly-used today. The latest version, the Harrier II, takes off from ships at sea as often as on land. The ship does not need to be an aircraft carrier, either. The Harrier is often launched from ships that normally just carry helicopters.

TECH TALK

The very first jump jet was actually a jump bed! Rolls-Royce engineers who first designed the special swivel engines used an old metal bed frame to test them. This flying bed was the great-grandfather of the Harrier!

TAKE-OFF

The single engine of a Harrier has four **nozzles**. The front nozzles are just behind the pilot, the rear ones are further back. All four nozzles face the rear for normal flight. To take off vertically or hover, the nozzles are pointed downwards.

This nozzle points downwards when the plane is taking off vertically or hovering.

INVISIBLE INTRUDERS

It is always best to surprise an enemy but aircraft can be seen by **radar**. This makes it very hard to surprise anyone at all. One way to escape radar is to fly close to the ground. This is called terrain masking, but it is very dangerous.

INVISIBLE BY DESIGN

A better way to hide from radar is to design an aircraft that is hard for radar to see. If a plane is just the right shape and covered with the right materials, radar is helpless! These invisible aircraft are called **stealth planes**.

The Lockheed F-117 Nighthawk is a stealth fighter. It has special features to keep it invisible.

B-2

The B-2 is the most expensive aircraft yet built. It can carry a huge bomb-load. Just imagine a whisper-quiet plane, which is nearly invisible to radar, but can carry mines, cruise missiles and nuclear bombs.

A parachute helps the F-117 slow down when landing.

HOW IT HIDES

- The spinning blades of a jet engine are simple for radar to see. The heat is also easy to detect. The engines of the F-117 are hidden deep inside the wings. The heat from the engines is mixed with cold air. This helps to keep the plane unseen.
- Weapons that hang under a wing are a simple shape for radar to see. The F-117 carries weapons inside its body. Only at the last moment are doors opened and the weapons fired.
- The edges of the F-117 are jagged when you are close up. This is because a jagged edge is harder to spot than a straight edge.

F-117

The F-117 stealth fighter is certainly a difficult plane to find or see. It was first seen in public in 1988, but had actually been flying secretly all over the world since 1982. And no one noticed!

45

ON PATROL

Patrol planes have an important job in wartime. They patrol the skies, watching out for the enemy. They may also go hunting for enemy ships or submarines.

EYES IN THE SKY

In peacetime their job is not as obvious but still very important. They help to patrol the seas and respond to emergencies. They are often used in search and rescue operations. They also watch over their country's borders. This helps to stop smugglers bringing in drugs, guns or diamonds.

The Nimrod is one of the best patrol aircraft ever built. It first flew in 1967 but is being upgraded to keep it flying until 2025.

THE ALBATROSS

This Russian Beriev A-40 is the largest seaplane flying today. It is also the only seaplane to be powered by **turbofans**. It has set many world records and is nicknamed The Albatross after the large, heavy seabird.

sonar buoy   floating equipment that detects sounds beneath the waves

EARS IN THE SKY

The Nimrod has two pilots and five crew. There are also four systems operators who use the Nimrod's hi-tech equipment. It is fitted with **radar**, magnetic detection equipment and sonar. With all this technology on board, the Nimrod can find things no other aircraft can.

In a search and rescue operation, the Nimrod is able to find ships, wreckage or survivors. It can guide other craft to whatever it finds. It can also drop survival equipment.

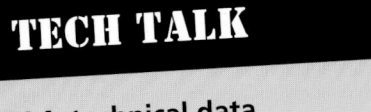

TECH TALK

Nimrod MRA4: technical data
- Length: 38.6 m
- Wingspan: 38.7 m
- Max. speed: 920 km/h (575 mph)
- Height: 9.45 m
- Weapons: AIM-9 Sidewinder, AGM-84 Harpoon anti-ship missiles, Stingray torpedoes, bombs, mines

SONAR

Sonar stands for SOund NAvigation and Ranging. It can detect things under water. It works by sending out a signal, or a 'ping'. If anything is out there, the signal reflects back and can be heard by the operator. Nimrods drop **sonar buoys** into the sea.

turbofan   type of jet engine; usually found on passenger aircraft

SPECIAL JETS

Concorde was the world's only **supersonic** airliner. The plane sped along at about 2173 km/h (1350 mph), which is much faster than other airliners. A trip from London to New York in Concorde took just three-and-a-half hours, instead of the normal eight hours.

WINGS AND BODY

Concorde had a curving wing. The fuel tanks were on the underside of the wing. The plane had a slim **fuselage**. The main cabin had a low ceiling, and room for just two seats on each side of the centre aisle. The airliner carried only 128 passengers and it was the most expensive airliner to fly on. A slower jet, such as the Boeing 747, has space for three times as many people.

BOEING SSBJ

This is the inside of the **prototype** of a small supersonic jet for business people. It might be built in the future.

TECH TALK

The nose of Concorde can be lowered during take-off.

BRITISH AIRWAYS

DROOPING NOSE

Concorde was one of only two airliners with a nose section that could be lowered. The Tu-144 Konkordski was the other jet that had this feature. Concorde took off and landed at a very high angle. Without the special drooping nose, the flight crew would not have been able to see out in front! The nose was raised for cruising flight.

HIGH FLIGHT

Concorde is a 'golden oldie' of the air. The first one flew in 1969. It has always been a favourite of the public. It still holds the record as the world's highest-flying airliner. It was retired from commercial use in 2003.

TECH TALK

The outside temperature on the tip of Concorde's nose can reach 127° Celsius. This is hotter than the temperature at which water boils, 100° Celsius.

KONKORDSKI

This Russian jet, designed in the 1960s, looked a bit like Concorde. It flew passengers in Russia but became too expensive to operate.

Concorde cruised at up to 18 kilometres (11 miles) above the ground.

COMMAND JETS

AWACS are a special sort of aircraft. AWACS stands for Airborne Warning And Control System. Without AWACS, military commanders would not know what is happening. The AWACS keep a watch on everything. They are also the centre for communication.

The Boeing E-3 Sentry is the most widely used AWACS jet in the world. More than 70 have been built.

EMBRAER COMMAND JET

This Embraer command jet is made in Brazil. Even though it is small compared to the Nimrod or E-3, it is still packed with electronic equipment. It is an excellent command jet for smaller air forces.

TECH TALK

AWACS radar can see everything around it in all directions. It has a range of 320 km (200 miles), and can track air, sea and land targets at the same time. It can tell the difference between friendly and enemy targets and works in any weather conditions.

The dish on top of the E-3 sends out radar signals.

headquarters   place from where things are planned and run

SPY IN THE SKY

The E-3 is a converted Boeing 707. The inside is very different, though. There are rows of computer screens and electronic equipment. The outside is different too, as the E-3 has a massive **radar** dish mounted above the **fuselage**. This dish turns every 10 seconds. The E-3 needs thirteen computer operators to use all the electronic equipment.

The E-3 flies very high and looks down on everything. It can be refuelled in the air. Nothing much is able to sneak past it.

E-8

The Northrop Grumman E-8 was first used during the 1991 Gulf War. It allowed commanders to see directly into enemy positions. They were also able to track their own forces at the same time.

TECH TALK

The E-4 is a special command jet. It is an airborne **headquarters**, in case everything on the ground is destroyed. It contains everything the US president needs to lead a country or command a war.

In an emergency, the E-4 becomes an airborne command centre.

AIR FORCE ONE

Air Force One is the jet that carries the president of the USA. It is a Boeing 747 but it has many extra features. It is sometimes called the Flying White House. The real White House is on the ground in Washington.

FLYING HQ

Air Force One has luxury cabins, bedrooms and rooms for the president's staff. There are rooms for news reporters and it is full of the most up-to-date technology.

The plane has anti-missile technology in case it is attacked. It also has incredible communications systems. It has a shield to stop nuclear blasts from wrecking the electronic systems. The jet even has a conference room, a fully equipped medical centre and a kitchen that can store up to 2000 meals.

WHAT IS AIR FORCE ONE?

Air Force One actually means any US Air Force plane that carries the president. When the president is not on board, the jet uses its normal **registration number**. If the president was on a B-52 or a Harrier jump jet, that plane would then become Air Force One.

The president even has use of a personal gym on board Air Force One.

registration number   set of letters and numbers used to identify vehicles

SAFE AND SECURE

In an emergency, the president could run the entire country from the sky if necessary. Air Force One has everything needed on board.

Air Force One can look after itself and needs little ground support. When it arrives in foreign countries it does not have to depend on people on the ground. It flies as part of a convoy. The other planes offer extra protection. Some of them carry security men, bullet-proof cars and sometimes the president's personal helicopter.

Air Force One has seen some amazing historic events. Decisions that have changed the world have been made on board. There is even a film about it!

ROYAL JET

The British Queen has her own jet aircraft. The Queen's Flight, a BAe 146, has been carefully converted and is full of incredible luxury. It also has hi-tech security systems. Members of the Royal Family sometimes fly the plane.

The Queen's Flight carries the Royal Family in style.

ROBOT FLYERS

Some jets do not have pilots at all. This happens when the jet has to carry out a dangerous task or when it is impossible for people to be present.

REMOTE CONTROL

Robot jets relay radio signals from space and control weather observation planes. They also map out the surface of the Earth or power spy planes. Robot jets can shoot down enemy planes or missiles.

Robot jets are also used to power missiles. The most famous of these missiles is the Tomahawk cruise missile.

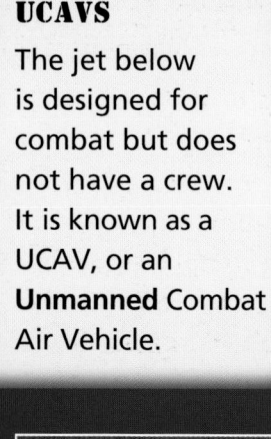

TECH TALK

Tomahawk cruise missile: technical data
- Length: 5.56 m
- Weight: 1587 kg
- Wingspan: 2.67 m
- Range: 1609 km (1006 miles)
- Speed: 880 km/h (550 mph)

MISSILE LAUNCH

Cruise missiles can be launched from ships, submarines and bomber airplanes. They are used to attack targets on the ground. These targets are usually heavily defended. It would be difficult for jet planes to reach these targets without being shot down.

COMPUTERS IN CONTROL

Cruise missiles fly very low. They have amazing guidance systems, which means they fly extremely fast but at rooftop level. Their small size, low **altitude** and high speeds make it hard for **radar** to spot them. They were first used in **combat** during the Gulf War in 1991 and were highly successful.

Cruise missiles can carry ordinary explosives as well as nuclear warheads.

PROTEUS

Proteus is a remote-controlled jet that can transmit television pictures and phone signals. It can also be used to relay Internet signals. The jet is solar powered, and the signals it sends are of excellent quality. In the future, it may be used to conduct atmospheric research.

STRANGE SHAPES

It can take a long time to take an aircraft from the planning stage to actual flight. Sometimes this can take as long as twenty years. Aircraft builders use **test-bed** planes to try out new ideas and technology.

FREAKY FLYERS

These planes can look very odd. The Boeing Bird of Prey is one of these peculiar jet aircraft. The Bird of Prey was top secret. It was used to test **stealth plane** designs in the 1990s. It flew 38 different test missions.

B-2 SPIRIT

Most people know this plane as a stealth bomber, but its full name is the Northrop Grumman B-2 Spirit. Buying one of these will not leave much change from a **billion** dollars.

The Bird of Prey was named after a spacecraft from *Star Trek*.

morphing changing shape

SUCCESS

The test flights were all successful. The technology that was tested on the Bird of Prey is now standard on many other aircraft. Because stealth technology is known around the world today, there is no need to keep the Bird of Prey a secret. It was shown to the public in 2002. The chairman of Boeing said: 'With this aircraft, we changed the rules on how to design and build.'

NEW IDEAS

Developers are experimenting with an incredible range of ideas. These include solar power and cleaner fuel, robot **combat** fighters and super-high **altitude** flying. These may well be used on the jets of the future!

MORPHING WING

The **morphing** wing concept is an experimental plane that changes wing-shape. It does this while it is actually flying. The idea is that the plane will alter its shape to suit the mission it has to carry out.

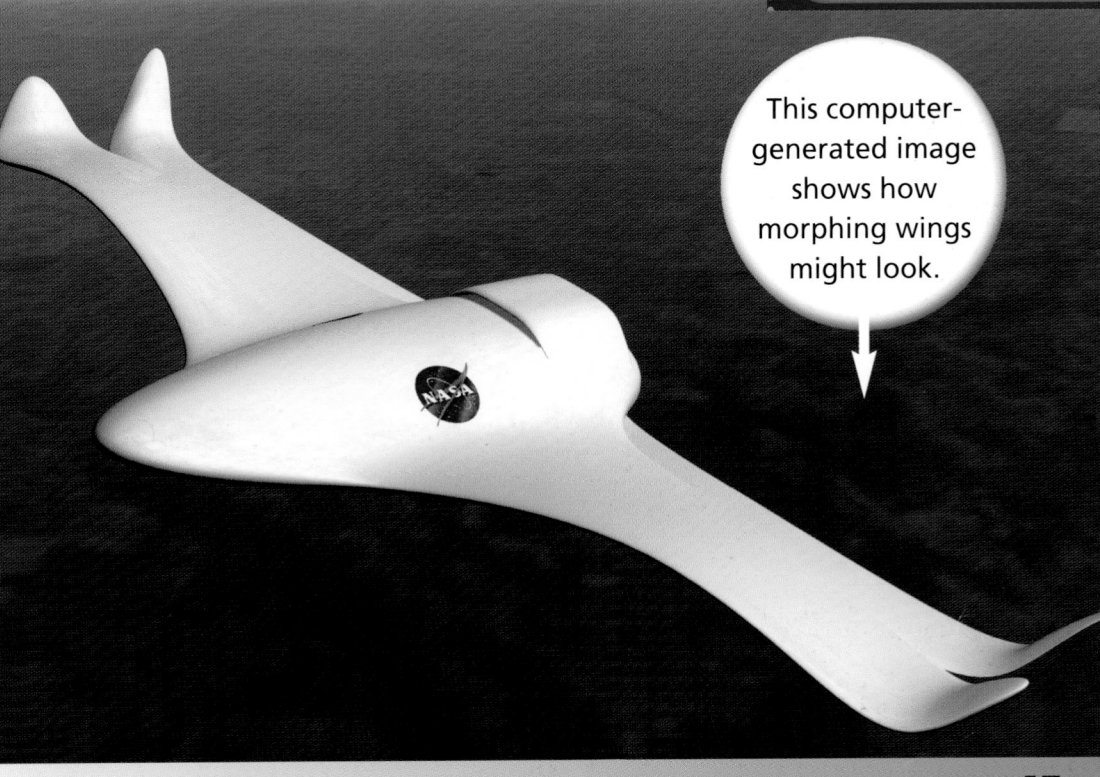

This computer-generated image shows how morphing wings might look.

JET FACTS

Busiest Airports, 2003			
Airport	**City**	**Country**	**Passengers**
Hartsfield-Jackson	Atlanta	USA	58,876,000
O'Hare International	Chicago	USA	51,832,000
Heathrow	London	UK	47,504,000
Tokyo International	Tokyo	Japan	47,320,000
Los Angeles International	Los Angeles	USA	41,289,000
Dallas-Fort Worth	Dallas	USA	39,389,000
Frankfurt International	Frankfurt	Germany	36,488,000
Charles de Gaulle	Paris	France	36,350,000
Schipol	Amsterdam	Holland	30,350,000
Sky Harbor International	Phoenix	USA	28,152,000

Largest Airliners	
Aircraft Model	**Maximum Passengers**
Airbus A-380-800	840
Boeing B-747-300	568
Boeing B-777-300	550
Airbus A-340-600	485
Airbus A-330-300	440
Boeing MD-11	410
Lockheed L-1011 TriStar	400
McDonnell Douglas DC-10-10	380
Boeing 767-400ER	375
Ilyushin Il-96	375

Air travel is one of the safest methods of transport. A person is more likely to die by drowning in a bath, falling from a ladder or freezing to death than by flying on a passenger jet.

Fastest Jets			
Date	**Jet**	**Speed**	
1946	Gloster Meteor F4	990.8 km/h	(615.7 mph)
1948	F-86 Sabre	1079.6 km/h	(670.8 mph)
1955	F-100 Super Sabre	1323 km/h	(822.1 mph)
1956	Fairey Delta 2	1821.8 km/h	(1132 mph)
1958	Lockheed F-104 Starfighter	2259.2 km/h	(1403.8 mph)
1961	McDonnell F-4 Phantom	2585.4 km/h	(1606.5 mph)
1965	Lockheed YF-12A Blackbird	3331.5 km/h	(2070.1 mph)
1967	North American X15	7274.2 km/h	(4520 mph)

If every engine were to break down on a passenger jet in mid-air, it may still be able to land. Most passenger jets can glide approximately 15 feet for each 1 foot they descend. An aeroplane flying at 30,000 feet can glide for about 135 kilometres (84 miles).

Have you ever seen a pilot with a thick beard? In the event of an air pressure problem, oxygen masks drop from the roof for passengers and crew to breathe through. Having a beard may stop the oxygen mask from fitting tightly.

FIND OUT MORE

BOOKS

Combat Aircraft (Collins, 2001)
Fighter Planes, Bill Gunston
(Ticktock Media, 1999)
Designed For Success: Attack Fighters,
Ian Graham (Heinemann Library, 2003)

WORLD WIDE WEB

If you want to find out more about jets you can search the Internet using keywords like these:

• 'US Air Force'
• turbine + engine
• jet + fighter

Make your own keywords using headings or words from this book. The search tips opposite will help you to find the most useful websites.

WEB SITES

X-PLANES
Read interviews with test pilots, look at great photographs of the most advanced jets and watch films that help explain the technology.
pbs.org/wgbh/ nova/xplanes

ROYAL AIR FORCE
Keep up to date with what the Air Force are doing. Lots of interesting information about the aircraft and weapons they use.
raf.mod.uk

BBC SCIENCE
Website packed with games and quizzes to find out about all aspects of science.
bbc.co.uk/science

SEARCH TIPS

There are billions of pages on the Internet so it can be difficult to find exactly what you are looking for. If you just type in 'jet' on a search engine like Google, you will get a list of 9 million web pages. These search skills will help you find useful websites more quickly.

- Use simple keywords, not whole sentences.
- Use two to six keywords in a search.
- Be precise – only use names of people, places or things.
- If you want to find words that go together, put quote marks around them, for example 'world speed record'.
- Use the advanced section of your search engine.
- Use the + sign between keywords to find pages with all these words.

WHERE TO SEARCH

SEARCH ENGINE

A search engine looks through the entire web and lists all sites that match the search words. The best matches are at the top of the list, on the first page. Try **bbc.co.uk/search**

SEARCH DIRECTORY

A search directory is like a library of websites. You can search by keyword or subject and browse through the different sites like you look through books on a library shelf. A good example is **yahooligans.com**

GLOSSARY

Air Cadets youth organization whose members learn about aircraft

altitude height above sea level

angle of attack how high the nose of the aircraft points upwards/downwards during flight

billion one thousand million

black out lose consciousness for a few seconds

cockpit in a combat aircraft, the place where the pilot sits

combat fighting

compressor part of a jet engine that squeezes the air going through the engine

decks floors

drag when air pushes back against an aircraft and slows it down

expand spread out and become larger in size

extinguisher fire-fighting cylinder kept on aircraft for emergencies

flight deck in a passenger aircraft, the place where the pilot sits

fuselage main body of an aircraft

G-force force of gravity that presses on pilots when they do sharp turns, steep climbs and dives

golden age great period in history

headquarters place from where things are planned and run

hydraulics strong equipment that uses liquid under pressure to move heavy parts of the airplane smoothly

jetliner jet plane built to carry passengers in comfort

Mach 1 the speed of sound

morphing changing shape

navigate / navigation planning and following a route

nozzle where compressed air comes out

private jet jet that you can buy or hire for your own use

propeller plane plane that is moved by a set of blades that spin round very quickly

prototype test version of a jet

radar (Radio Detection and Ranging) way of seeing other planes when they are many miles away

registration number set of letters and numbers used to identify vehicles

signal beacon device that sends out an emergency radio signal

simulator a training machine that imitates flight

sonar buoys floating equipment that detects sounds beneath the waves

sonic boom noise heard when an aircraft passes by at a speed faster than Mach 1

sound barrier drag and other problems that make a plane hard to control when it gets close to the speed of sound

stall when a plane goes too slowly and cannot maintain height

stealth plane aircraft that is difficult to detect with radar

stick control lever that changes the direction of a plane

streamlined / streamlining designed to move easily through the air

strobe light powerful flashing light used to signal for help

supersonic faster than the speed of sound

test-bed aircraft built only to test parts and experiment with new designs

throttle used by a pilot to control engine power

thrust force produced by a jet engine to push a plane forward

turbine part of a jet engine that is used to power the big fan at the front of the engine

turbofan jet engine where a fan mixes air into the engine; these engines are larger but quieter and usually found on passenger aircraft

turbojet more basic type of jet engine

unmanned without a crew or pilot

unstable likely to go wrong

vapour trail white trail left in the sky by a jet

vertical straight up (and down)

wind tunnel place where testing can be done on speed and conditions

Raintree would like to thank the following for information used in this book: Airports Council International, Air Transport Intelligence.

INDEX